PROPERTY OF

Hartshorne Public Library
720 Pennsylvania Avenue
Hartshorne, OK 74547

SOUTHEASTERN PUBLIC LIBRARY SYSTEM OF OKLAHOMA

P9-ASL-990

J 576.8 OBRIEN
O'Brien, Cynthia (Cynthia J.).
Searching for extraterrestrials.

2019
02/08/2019

482936908   50792571622902   COM9183680
SEARCHING FOR EXTRAT   CODE39
0023911972   001718   214561L4220274000000

Searching for Extraterrestrials

Cynthia O'Brien

CRABTREE
PUBLISHING COMPANY
WWW.CRABTREEBOOKS.COM

Author: Cynthia O'Brien

Editors: Sarah Eason, Tim Cooke, Ellen Rodger

Editorial director: Kathy Middleton

Design: Paul Myerscough, Lynne Lennon

Cover design: Paul Myerscough

Photo research: Rachel Blount

Proofreader and indexer: Nancy Dickmann, Wendy Scavuzzo

Production coordinator and prepress technician: Ken Wright

Print coordinator: Katherine Berti

Consultant: David Hawksett

Produced for Crabtree Publishing by Calcium Creative

Photo Credits:
t=Top, tr=Top Right, tl=Top Left

Inside: NASA: p. 21; Observatory images from NASA, ESA (Herschel and Planck), Lavochkin Association (Specktr-R), HESS Collaboration (HESS), Salt Foundation (SALT), Rick Peterson/WMKO (Keck), Germini Observatory/AURA (Gemini), CARMA team (CARMA), and NRAO/AUI (Greenbank and VLA); background image from NASA): p. 28; NASA/GSFC/METI/ERSDAC/JAROS, and U.S./Japan ASTER Science Team: p. 25; NASA Goddard: pp. 41, 42; NASA/Tony Gray: p. 18; NASA/Leif Heimbold: p. 19; NASA/JPL-Caltech: pp. 1, 4, 14, 15, 16, 27, 30; NASA/JPL-Caltech/ASU: p. 13; NASA/JPL-Caltech/MSSS: pp. 31, 43; NASA/JPL-Caltech/USGS: pp. 11, 32; Shutterstock: 3Dstock: p. 23; Jose Arcos Aguilar: p. 20; Paulo Afonso: p. 29; AlexHliv: p. 44; Sheri Armstrong: p. 34; John M. Chase: p. 17; Curioso: p. 6; Daa.riaa: p. 24; Massimo Dallaglio: p. 5; FOTOKITA: p. 39; Brian P Irwin: p. 8; Andrea Izzotti: p. 10; Liz Kcer: p. 38; Yuriy Mazur: p. 35; Natrot: p. 7; Nerthuz: p. 45; SipaPhoto: p. 37; Keith Tarrier: p. 36; Wikimedia Commons: NASA: p. 40; NASA, ESA, and M. Livio and the Hubble 20th Anniversary Team (STScI): p. 33; NOAA: p. 26; Jim Peaco, National Park Service: p. 22; Republic: p. 9.

Cover: Shutterstock: Zack Frank.

Library and Archives Canada Cataloguing in Publication

O'Brien, Cynthia (Cynthia J.), author
    Searching for extraterrestrials / Cynthia O'Brien.

(Mission: space science)
Includes index.
Issued in print and electronic formats.
ISBN 978-0-7787-5394-0 (hardcover).--
ISBN 978-0-7787-5405-3 (softcover).--
ISBN 978-1-4271-2209-4 (HTML)

    1. Life on other planets--Juvenile literature.
2. Extraterrestrial beings--Juvenile literature.
3. Outer space--Exploration--Juvenile literature. I. Title.

QB54.O27 2019   j576.8'39   C2018-906108-1
                                   C2018-906109-X

Library of Congress Cataloging-in-Publication Data

Names: O'Brien, Cynthia (Cynthia J.), author.
Title: Searching for extraterrestrials / Cynthia O'Brien.
Description: New York, New York : Crabtree Publishing, [2019] |
  Series: Mission: space science | Includes index.
Identifiers: LCCN 2018050349 (print) |
  LCCN 2018052348 (ebook) |
  ISBN 9781427122094 (Electronic) |
  ISBN 9780778753940 (hardcover) |
  ISBN 9780778754053 (pbk.)
Subjects: LCSH: Life on other planets--Juvenile literature. |
  Exobiology--Juvenile literature. | Space sciences--
  Juvenile literature.
Classification: LCC QB54 (ebook) |
  LCC QB54 .O235 2019 (print) | DDC 576.8/39--dc23
LC record available at https://lccn.loc.gov/2018050349

Crabtree Publishing Company

www.crabtreebooks.com   1-800-387-7650

Printed in the U.S.A./032019/CG20190118

Copyright © **2019 CRABTREE PUBLISHING COMPANY.** All rights reserved. No part of this publication may be reproduced, stored in a retrieval system or be transmitted in any form or by any means, electronic, mechanical, photocopying, recording, or otherwise, without the prior written permission of Crabtree Publishing Company. In Canada: We acknowledge the financial support of the Government of Canada through the Canada Book Fund for our publishing activities.

Published in Canada
Crabtree Publishing
616 Welland Ave.
St. Catharines, Ontario
L2M 5V6

Published in the United States
Crabtree Publishing
PMB 59051
350 Fifth Avenue, 59th Floor
New York, New York 10118

Published in the United Kingdom
Crabtree Publishing
Maritime House
Basin Road North, Hove
BN41 1WR

Published in Australia
Crabtree Publishing
Unit 3 – 5
Currumbin Court
Capalaba QLD 4157

Contents

For thousands of years, people have wondered if there is life beyond Earth. For more than 100 years, scientists have been trying to answer that question. People on Earth are **terrestrials**, a word that comes from the Latin *terra*, which means "earth" or "land." An **extraterrestrial** is a life form that exists beyond Earth.

Our Solar System

Astronomers are scientists who study the stars, **planets**, and other aspects of space. Some astronomers are searching for life beyond our planet. Earth is one of eight planets in our **Solar System**. This is a system in which planets **orbit**, or travel around, a star. Earth's star is the Sun. Astronomers are studying these other planets and their moons, but the search does not end there. Our Solar System is part of a spiral-shaped **galaxy** called the Milky Way. Our Solar System lies within one curved part of the spiral, called the Orion Arm.

Earth's Solar System belongs to a spiral galaxy, or collection of stars, similar to this galaxy, M33.

Radio telescopes scan space for signals that might be signs that intelligent life exists elsewhere in the universe.

There may be as many as 400 billion stars in the galaxy. Many of these stars have at least one planet orbiting them. This means that there are billions of possible places for scientists to look for life in the Milky Way alone. There are billions of other galaxies in the universe, and they also have billions of stars orbited by planets.

Extraterrestrial Experts

Earth's galaxy is so vast that many people believe that life must exist somewhere in it other than on Earth. What kind of life could this be? Extraterrestrials may take a form that we do not recognize. **Astrobiologists** are scientists who are looking for extraterrestrial life. They study the beginnings and future of life in the universe, as well as its **evolution** and **distribution**, or where it is found.

Astrobiology has become an important part of space science. In 1998, the National Aeronautics and Space Administration (NASA) established the NASA Astrobiology Institute (NAI) to search for signs of life.

One part of astrobiology is the search for intelligent life. Its scientists are looking for signs of thinking life forms in the universe. In the late 1970s, NASA began the Search for Extraterrestrial Intelligence (SETI). The SETI Institute, founded in 1984, is a leading research center that works with NASA.

NASA and the SETI Institute are two leading U.S. organizations, but the search for extraterrestrial life involves astrobiologists, astronomers, engineers, and many others around the world. Together, they may find it.

The idea of extraterrestrial life is not new. More than 2,000 years ago, the ancient Greek **philosopher**, or thinker, Epicurus wrote that there were "infinite worlds both like and unlike ours." He also believed that some form of life existed in these worlds.

Ancient peoples did not have the technology that we possess today. They did not know that the Sun was a star, or that Earth is part of a solar system. In 1532, astronomer Nicolaus Copernicus became the first person to describe in a scientific way how Earth and the other planets orbited the Sun. This suggested that, if Earth could support life, it seemed likely that other planets could, too.

Lights and Mirrors

In the 1800s, people began to look for ways to send messages to extraterrestrials. Carl Gauss, a German mathematician, had the idea of using a **heliotrope**. A heliotrope was a device that used mirrors to reflect sunlight over long distances. It was used to measure land. Gauss believed a giant heliotrope could reflect sunlight to the Moon. However, Gauss never built the heliotrope. By the 1900s, the idea of "Martians," or beings living on Mars, had taken hold of people's imaginations and they began to develop more ideas for sending signals into space. These included sending flashes of reflected electric light and putting mirrors on top of the Eiffel Tower in Paris, France.

Nicolaus Copernicus's theory that Earth orbited the Sun went against the previously held idea that the Sun and planets orbited Earth.

> Radio waves are a form of electromagnetic radiation. They are invisible, but transfer energy from one place to another.

Radio Waves

Radio waves are disturbances that travel through space in the same way that waves travel through water, in a series of up and down movements. Many types of communications use radio waves, from radios and cell phones to telescopes. In the late 1800s, Nicola Tesla and Guglielmo Marconi pioneered using radio waves to send messages. In 1901, Tesla claimed to have picked up strange signals that he believed were a message from extraterrestrials. Twenty years later, Marconi also reported receiving signals from space. In 1933, the U.S. astronomer Karl Jansky discovered that some objects in space do indeed produce radio waves. The Sun, for example, produces radio waves. Studying radio waves is called radio astronomy. Today, it is an important way to study space and search for extraterrestrials.

YOUR MISSION

Many scientists believe that the chances of finding extraterrestrial life in the universe are high. What arguments would you use to persuade people that a mission to find extraterrestrial life is worth pursuing?

The search for extraterrestrial life picked up dramatically in the 1950s. "Aliens" became the subject of books, movies, and television series. This was **science fiction**, or stories based on an imaginary future with advanced technology. At the same time, astronomers, engineers, and other scientists were looking at real ways to explore space.

Finding other forms of life in the universe became the subject of serious scientific research. In 1959, the astronomers Giuseppe Cocconi and Philip Morrison published a paper called "Searching for Interstellar Communication." The authors suggested using electromagnetic signals to communicate with extraterrestrials. This sparked the modern search for intelligent extraterrestrial life.

The Space Race

In the 1960s, a "space race" began as the Soviet Union and the United States each tried to prove their technological superiority. In 1957, the Soviets launched Sputnik, a **satellite** that orbited Earth.

In January 1958, the United States launched its own satellite, Explorer 1. In July, the U.S. government established NASA to run its space program. Just over a decade later, in 1969, the U.S. Apollo 11 mission landed the first humans on the Moon.

The space race sparked great public interest in space travel and the possibility of alien life. In 1966, the astronomers Carl Sagan and Iosif Shklovskii published *Intelligent Life in the Universe*. The book explained why some astronomers believed life could exist on other planets.

The telescope at Arecibo in Puerto Rico opened in 1963. It uses a huge dish built into the ground to collect radio waves.

Difficult Calculation

Like Cocconi and Morrison, the U.S. astronomer Frank Drake believed humans should try to communicate with extraterrestrials. In 1960, his first search for extraterrestrials began with Project Ozma. He hoped that the large radio telescope at the National Radio Astronomy **Observatory** at Green Bank, West Virginia, would detect signals from intelligent life in space. The telescope did not pick up anything, but Drake's research led to his mapping of the center of the Milky Way and other important discoveries.

In 1961, Drake came up with an **equation**, or calculation, for estimating how many extraterrestrial **civilizations** might exist. It was based on factors such as the number of stars that might have planets, the number of planets that might harbor life, and how long life would take to develop civilizations.

More recent astronomers questioned the usefulness of the Drake equation. Many believe, however, that the sheer number of stars and planets in the universe suggests that life probably exists elsewhere. The distances involved are so huge, however, that it may never be possible to make contact.

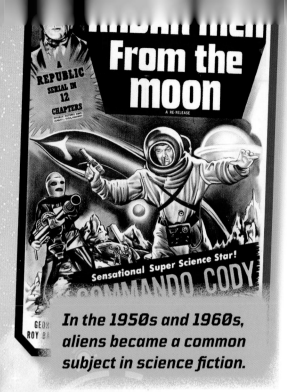

In the 1950s and 1960s, aliens became a common subject in science fiction.

MISSION:

Space Science

Project Ozma used a giant 85-foot (26 m) radio telescope with a receiver attached. Frank Drake and his team aimed the telescope at two stars, about 11 **light-years** away from Earth. They set the receiver to scan for any incoming messages. For two months, the team looked for a series of pulses or **prime numbers**. The receiver did not find any messages, but this was the start of SETI as a serious science.

Looking For Life

All living things on Earth have basic needs that must be met in order for them to survive. If life beyond Earth exists, would these living things have the same needs? Scientists are looking for clues. If any forms of extraterrestrial life exist, intelligent life may also be possible.

Signs of Life

Earth is home to a wide range of life. Some are tiny, simple **organisms** but others are more complex life forms, such as plants and animals, including human beings. All forms of life have the same basic requirements, such as water and food to provide energy, so life is only likely to exist on a planet that has conditions that meet those needs. Another basic requirement is **carbon**, which is an **element** that occurs in all living things. Astrobiologists looking for life beyond Earth look for "**biosignatures**." These are pieces of evidence that suggest that a planet has the conditions to support life, such as carbon-based molecules. Without carbon, there is unlikely to be life.

All forms of life, from germs to playful dolphins, require carbon, water, and a source of energy.

Astrobiologists look for gases such as oxygen and methane, which occur naturally but can also be produced by life forms. Such gases may be a sign that life could exist on another planet. At the same time, however, the combinations of chemicals needed for life may not be quite the same on another planet. Life forms may look different, too.

Intelligent Life

Astrobiologists who are looking for intelligent life face further problems. How do they define intelligence? On Earth, some animals have the ability to solve problems or use tools. Humans have created advanced technologies. Perhaps intelligent extraterrestrial life depends on this ability. Astrobiologists focus on **multicellular** life forms, but what if extraterrestrials are machines? Machines are not alive, but can possess **artificial intelligence (AI)**, which is an ability to process information in a form similar to thinking in humans.

Goldilocks Worlds

The fairy tale about Goldilocks and the three bears is about things being just right. Astrobiologists search for what they call Goldilocks worlds, which are planets that are just right to support

Titan, the largest moon of Saturn, has lakes of liquid methane and ethane. It is possible that some form of life exists on Titan.

life. Earth is a good size for living things. Other planets may be too small to maintain an **atmosphere** that would protect life. Planets that are too large could have an atmosphere so dense it would crush life forms. Temperature is important, too. Planets that orbit too close to their star, such as Venus, are too hot. Planets that are too far away, such as Neptune, are too cold.

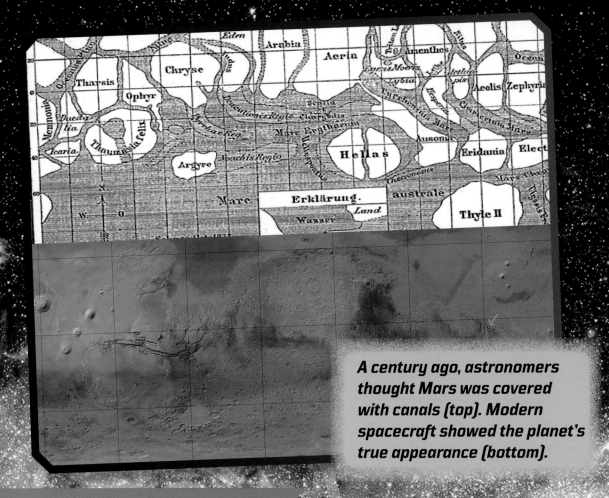

A century ago, astronomers thought Mars was covered with canals (top). Modern spacecraft showed the planet's true appearance (bottom).

Life on Mars?

After Venus, the next closest planet to Earth is Mars. As the two planets travel around the Sun, they come within 35.8 million miles (57.6 million km) of each other. That is still a vast distance, but since the 1960s, astronomers have sent spacecraft to explore Mars. In recent decades, vehicles called **rovers** have allowed scientists to explore the surface of Mars close-up.

Traces of Water

In the 1870s, Italian astronomer Giovanni Schiaparelli studied Mars through a telescope. Schiaparelli claimed to see channels on Mars he called "canali." This seemed to indicate either that there might be water on Mars, or that it had once existed there. In 1894, the U.S. astronomer Percival Lowell took this idea further.

Lowell built a telescope in Arizona to map the "canals" on Mars. He believed the channels were canals built by intelligent Martians. Today, we know the canals do not exist, but missions to Mars have found evidence that the planet once had water. This means that some form of life may have existed on Mars millions of years ago.

Gathering Evidence

In 1971, NASA launched Mariner 9, the first spacecraft to orbit Mars. The photographs Mariner 9 sent back to Earth revealed vast canyons that must have been formed by rivers that once flowed on Mars. NASA sent the Viking lander spacecraft in 1976 to look for signs of life on the surface. The landers found some chemical activity in the soil, but no sign of life. Since that time, a series of rovers have explored Mars's surface. Curiosity landed on Mars in 2012. It sent back information about the layers of rock and soil in the planet's Gale **Crater** that showed the crater had once held a large lake. This means life could have existed on Mars in the past, maybe for a long time.

MISSION:

Space Science

Information from NASA's rovers provided evidence that water once existed on Mars. In June 2018, the rover Curiosity uncovered larger **organic** molecules than had been found on Mars before. Some of the molecules are similar to those in coal. The rover found these carbon-based organic molecules in rock that was 3.5 billion years old. The rock was heated to a very high temperature to release the molecules. Future missions could drill deeper into the rock and discover more organic material.

Since 2012, the Curiosity rover has explored a large indent on Mars called the Gale Crater.

In 1992, astronomers discovered two planets orbiting a star. These are extra-solar planets, or **exoplanets**, which exist outside our Solar System. Three years later, Swiss astronomers found another exoplanet orbiting a star similar to the Sun. The star was 51 Pegasi, which is about 42 light-years from Earth, and astronomers named the exoplanet 51 Pegasi b. The exoplanet is very large and gassy. It is about half the size of Jupiter, the largest planet in our Solar System. Astronomers went on to find many similar exoplanets. They estimated that most stars have at least four planets. This means that many billions of exoplanets may exist.

Types of Exoplanets

There are icy exoplanets, rocky ones, and large, gassy ones. Most known exoplanets are larger than Earth and are outside the **habitable zone**, where life is possible in a planetary system. They are either too close or too far away from the star to support life. At just the right distance, an exoplanet may be **habitable**, or have the potential for life. These planets may be rocky, like Earth, and have water, the key to life.

Habitable-zone exoplanets fall into three main types. "Subterran" exoplanets are smaller than Earth. "Terran" exoplanets are Earth-size.

K2-33b is one of the youngest exoplanets yet discovered. It orbits its young star every five days.

The exoplanets orbiting TRAPPIST-1 seem to be rocky, and three are in their solar system's habitable zone.

"Super-terran" exoplanets are larger than Earth. The most common type, super Earths, are two to three times the size of Earth. Research suggests some super Earths may have thicker atmospheres that could help protect any life forms. The University of Puerto Rico keeps a list of all exoplanets at the Planetary Habitability Laboratory in Arecibo. The Habitable Exoplanets Catalog lists all of the exoplanets and what we know about them.

Latest Discoveries

By 2018, scientists had discovered more than 3,740 exoplanets. They also have evidence that suggests many more exist, but the evidence has to be carefully checked. In 2016, scientists using a space telescope in Chile found three Earth-sized exoplanets. A year later, scientists using the NASA Spitzer telescope announced that they had found seven planets orbiting a star known as TRAPPIST-1. Exploring these exoplanets may bring exciting news about extraterrestrial life.

YOUR MISSION

From what you have read in this book, what kinds of exoplanets might be the most likely places to discover extraterrestrial life? Does another planet need to be just like Earth, or could it be completely different?

The Kepler space telescope was launched in 2009. Its mission was to study and record information about a group of 100,000 stars. Kepler orbits Earth searching for exoplanets, and particularly for Earthlike ones. One of these exoplanets may have evidence of extraterrestrial life.

Discoveries

In its first year, Kepler discovered five exoplanets. In 2013, Kepler suffered from technical problems, but engineers figured out a remarkable way to use sunlight to make the telescope operate again. After this, the Kepler mission became known as Kepler 2, or K2. It continued its search.

In April 2014, K2 discovered the first Earthlike exoplanet, known as Kepler-186f. Could there be life on Kepler-186f? The exoplanet is about 500 light-years away, so humans will not be visiting it any time soon. Another Kepler discovery, Kepler-452b, also seems very similar to Earth. It takes 385 days to orbit its host star, while Earth takes 365 days to orbit the Sun. Kepler-452, the planet's star, is 6 billion years old,

which is 1.5 billion years older than our Sun. This exoplanet is 1,400 light-years away from Earth, so it is difficult to learn more about it. SETI scientists are aiming their equipment at Kepler-452b to search for signs of life.

Kepler-186f

ER SIDE

This poster is one of a series NASA produced that treats places in the universe as tourist destinations.

Hunt for Signals

As astrobiologists look for biosignatures, SETI scientists search for "**technosignatures**." These are radio waves that could not come from natural sources. The Kepler mission has helped identify places to look for these signals. However, technosignatures are difficult to identify. What seem to be technosignatures are often the result of interference from satellites. In 2018, NASA announced that K2 was about to run out of fuel. Other missions will take over and explore further.

The Kepler space telescope has detected many exoplanets using the **transit method**. The telescope monitors a star's light over a period of time. When a planet orbits around its star, it "transits," or passes in front of it. Scientists look to see how much light the planet blocks. This allows them to estimate the planet's size and how long it takes to orbit its star.

SETI scientists use the world's largest steerable radio telescope in Green Bank, West Virginia, to look for technosignatures.

Exoplanet Survey

NASA's Transiting Exoplanet Survey Satellite (TESS) has a specific mission. Launched in April 2018, it was designed to search for planets around the nearest, brightest stars. These are stars that are fewer than 300 light-years from Earth. They are dim, **red dwarf** stars. They are cooler than our Sun, which means that exoplanets can orbit closer to their stars. TESS will circle Earth every 13.7 days and send back data to the surface.

TESS will explore a far larger area than the Kepler missions. Over two years, TESS will monitor more than 200,000 stars in an area that is 400 times larger than Kepler's territory. TESS is equipped with four cameras. Each camera can view a large area of the sky. TESS will study each area for about 27 days before moving on. TESS is looking for exoplanets close to Earth, so it may be easier to identify signs of life there than on more distant ones.

TESS takes off from Florida in April 2018 onboard a SpaceX Falcon 9 rocket.

On the Ground

TESS is a NASA mission, but it is operated by the Massachusetts Institute of Technology (MIT). It also involves other partners, such as the Harvard-Smithsonian Center for Astrophysics. Many scientists and engineers on the ground work to study and follow up on the information that TESS sends back to Earth.

As TESS identifies exoplanets, teams on the ground will check them. They will use telescopes to obtain images of these TESS Objects of Interest (TOIs). The ground team will use a method called **radial velocity** to find exoplanets. Radial velocity looks for a star to "wobble" as it is pulled by a planet's **gravity**. The size of the wobble in the star's energy indicates the size of the planet. Putting all the information together, scientists can figure out if the planets are gassy, watery, or rocky, like Earth. The TESS mission team members expect the satellite to find between 100 and 200 Earth-sized worlds, in addition to thousands of other exoplanets.

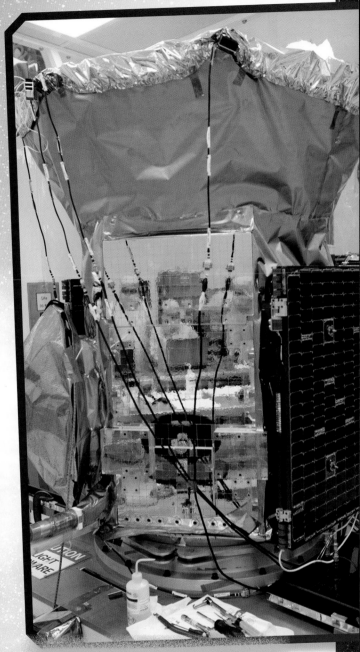

TESS is about the size of a refrigerator. It carries four cameras to detect exoplanets.

CHAPTER 3

Clues on Earth

Life on Earth began 3.5 billion years ago as simple, tiny life forms were created by chemical reactions. It took billions of years for more complex life forms, such as plants and animals, to evolve. Life on other planets may look the same as life on Earth, or it may be quite different from what we are used to. However, a close look at life on Earth is a good place to start considering the nature of any kind of extraterrestrial life.

Earth has a wide variety of environments, from salty oceans to dry deserts. There are boiling hot volcanoes and large stretches of ice. Astrobiologists study these extreme environments because they also occur on other planets and moons. If it is impossible to look at locations in space up close, these similar environments are the next best thing. These places on Earth may provide information about life on other worlds.

The Tinto River in Spain is dyed red by minerals. Similar conditions might have existed if there was ever water on Mars.

The barren Atacama Desert in Chile might be similar to conditions on other planets.

There are many examples of extreme environments on Earth. The water in the Tinto River in Spain, for example, is red from iron and sulfur, like the surface of Mars. The environment around the river is very **acidic**, so few animals or plants can survive near it. During the Mars Analog Research and Technology Experiment on the river, scientists found life. Astrobiologists have studied caves on Earth full of poisonous gases. They have also explored the icy landscapes of Antarctica and the Arctic.

Earth History

Earth formed about 4.5 billion years ago, but it took time for life to develop. Studying the timeline of life on Earth helps astrobiologists understand how life might develop on other planets.

They look at how living organisms developed from nonliving materials, such as water and rock, and how long it took. This is why the age of a planet is important. On newer planets, we may find the beginnings of life. On older planets, life as we know it may be gone. After all, modern humans have only been around about 200,000 years. That is a short time in the history of life on Earth.

At the same time, astrobiologists remain aware that life may develop differently on other planets. If extraterrestrial life does not need carbon, what other combinations of gases or chemical systems might produce life? Biologists have already learned that life on Earth sometimes comes in very surprising forms.

It seems impossible that anything can live on Earth in environments that are very hot, very cold, or extreme in other ways. Somehow, however, life is able to exist even in the most hostile environments on the planet. Scientists call these organisms **extremophiles**, which means they like extreme conditions. They classify them according to the conditions in which they survive. Studying these life forms can help astrobiologists to better understand what kinds of life might exist in extreme conditions in space.

Types of Life

There are nine different kinds of extremophiles on Earth:

· **Thermophiles** survive in extreme heat, such as temperatures that exist in the inside of an active volcano.

· **Radioresistant microbes** cope with levels of radiation that humans could not survive.

· **Barophiles** live in high-pressure places, such as the bottom of the ocean.

· **Psychrophiles** are cold lovers. Many have a special "antifreeze" that keeps them from freezing.

· **Xerophiles** exist in very dry places where there is little water.

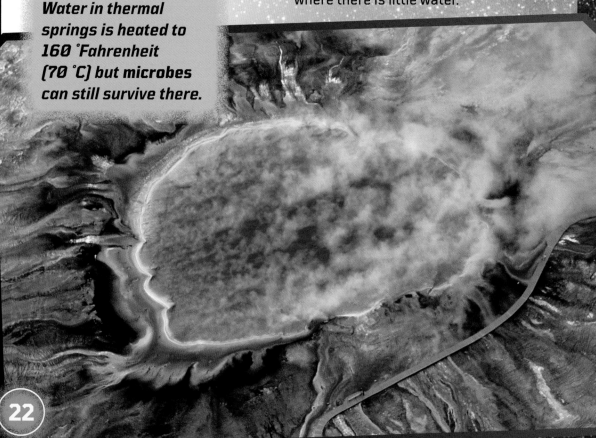

Water in thermal springs is heated to 160 °Fahrenheit (70 °C) but microbes can still survive there.

- **Alkaliphiles** have adapted to high **alkaline** environments. Alkaline chemicals neutralize or balance acids.
- **Acidophiles** might be found in places of high acid, such as waste-treatment plants.
- **Halophiles** like extremely salty environments.
- **Endoliths** can live in rock or deep inside the Earth.

Tardigrades

The best survivors scientists have discovered on Earth are **tardigrades**, which are sometimes called "water bears." Tardigrades seem to be able to live anywhere, from extreme heat or cold to places with high radiation or crushing pressures. They are tiny, eight-legged creatures, about 0.04 inches (1 mm) long. In extreme conditions, tardigrades go into a **dehydrated** state and curl into an almost lifeless ball. They can stay like this for many years and still come back to life.

In 2007, tardigrades survived a trip into space. The European Space Agency (ESA) sent tardigrades into space on the outside of a satellite. After 10 days, the satellite returned to Earth. Despite having no protection from radiation or high pressure, many of the tardigrades survived and even laid eggs to increase the population.

The tardigrade was first discovered by using a microscope in 1773.

YOUR MISSION

Knowing what you have read about exoplanets and their conditions, what kinds of life might exist on these planets? How might these life forms evolve? Think about the age of exoplanets. Some are much older than Earth. Others are younger. How would this affect what life forms exist there?

Scientists believe conditions in parts of Antarctica are similar to those on other planets.

Ice Cold

Earth's coldest places give us clues to life long ago on our own planet. They also tell us what types of life might exist on cold planets or moons. Astrobiologists have studied Antarctica, in particular. This icy world is a dry, cold, dark desert. There are no plants. The only people are scientists who live in research stations. There are no towns or cities. Animals, such as penguins, live on the edges of Antarctica where they can find food in the sea. Elsewhere, only extremophiles seem to survive.

McMurdo Dry Valleys

One of the areas of Antarctica that astrobiologists study is much like the surface of Mars. The McMurdo Dry Valleys is a large, almost ice-free region of Antarctica. The valleys are home to **colonies** of **bacteria**, which are simple, microscopic forms of life. Researchers have found bacteria living in the rocks. Even more interesting is that salty, underground water may help life exist under the surface. The evidence of the water is in a very shallow, salty pond.

There is also salty water on Mars and on moons such as Europa, which orbits Jupiter, and Enceladus, which orbits Saturn. The studies in Antarctica show that life can still exist in extremely cold, salty environments like these.

Lake Life

Antarctica's Lake Whillans lies beneath half a mile (0.8 km) of ice. It is one of hundreds of similar lakes. It has been covered by ice for about 1 million years. Scientists used a hot-water drill to discover almost 4,000 microbe species in the buried lake. Without energy from the Sun, these microbes have to find other ways to live. Researchers plan to study other ice-covered lakes that may have different conditions. What conditions might extraterrestrial life need? For example, in 2017, scientists discovered a new bacterium near the east coast of Antarctica. This unusual organism survives on hydrogen, carbon monoxide, and carbon dioxide in the air.

The McMurdo Dry Valleys of Antarctica is a fascinating region for astrobiologists.

Many exoplanets are very hot. The hottest Earth environments range from dry, sun-baked deserts to the ocean floor. In 1965, the first extremophiles were found in hot springs in Yellowstone National Park in the United States. The bacteria live in super-hot water rising from inside Earth.

Deep beneath the ocean, hot water from inside Earth shoots up through **hydrothermal vents**, which are cracks in the ocean floor. The water is full of chemicals and minerals that would kill most living things. In this hot, dark world, colonies of thermophiles thrive. **Tubeworms** live off the bacteria. These creatures live in the very deep sea, where there is no sunlight at all. Their food energy comes only from the vents.

Earth's Hot Spot

The Danakil Depression in Ethiopia is one of the hottest, lowest, driest places on Earth. It is part of the East African Great Rift Valley.

Hydrothermal vents are sometimes called black smokers. They release mineral-rich water at temperatures of up to 867 ˚Fahrenheit (464 ˚C).

This extreme environment is of great interest to astrobiologists. As well as being extremely hot, the Danakil Depression gets very little rain, and it is very acidic and salty. It is an area of active volcanoes. The air contains poisonous gases such as chlorine and sulfur dioxide. Its hot springs are bright yellow and its **lava**, or molten rock, burns blue. The area still needs study, but expeditions have already found extremophiles living there.

MISSION:
Space Science

A 2018 and 2019 NASA mission took researchers into the deep sea. The Systematic Underwater Biogeochemical Science and Exploration Analog (SUBSEA) mission studied an undersea volcano 3,000 feet (915 m) below the surface of the ocean near Hawaii. The conditions there are similar to what might exist on Saturn's moon, Enceladus, and Jupiter's moon, Europa. As in space, explorers used **remotely operated vehicles (ROVs)**. These are robots that are controlled from far away. For the SUBSEA mission, underwater robots were controlled by scientists onboard a ship. The life forms they found may give clues to the kinds of life that might live on these watery moons.

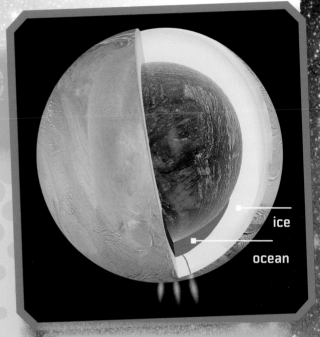

ice

ocean

In this illustration, water vapor and ice jet from the southern pole of Enceladus, which has a shell of ice over an interior ocean.

CHAPTER 4

Exploration Tools

Looking for life in the universe requires a wide range of tools on Earth and in space. Giant radio telescopes search for signals, while rovers have landed on Mars to explore its surface. Instruments such as these help astronomers study objects that would be impossible to visit. The nearest exoplanet is more than 4 light-years from Earth. That is about 25 trillion miles (40 trillion km). Even with the remarkable technology we have today, this planet would take many thousands of years to reach.

Looking at Space

The human eye can see only some of what is out in space. The nearest stars are so far away that their light takes years to reach Earth. The electromagnetic **spectrum** contains many types of energy waves that humans cannot see. These include radio waves, microwaves, infrared radiation, ultraviolet radiation, X-rays, and gamma rays. Radio waves are low-energy waves that travel at the speed of light. Unlike visible light waves, they can travel through the dust-filled galaxy.

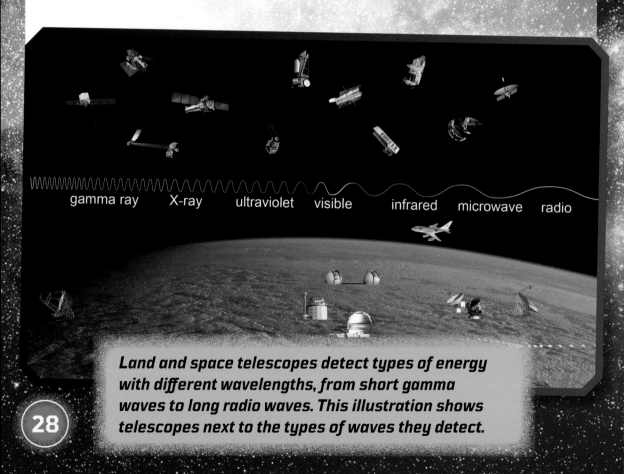

gamma ray   X-ray   ultraviolet   visible   infrared   microwave   radio

Land and space telescopes detect types of energy with different wavelengths, from short gamma waves to long radio waves. This illustration shows telescopes next to the types of waves they detect.

SETI owns the Allen Telescope Array at Hat Creek in California.

Radio Telescopes

Radio waves from space can reveal a lot about the stars and planets. Astronomers measure the length or frequency of the waves. Computers turn this invisible light into images that can be studied. Radio telescopes collect radio waves from space using one or more **antennae**. Often, they are shaped like a big, curved dish. Receivers and **amplifiers** help boost the signals. The information is sent to a computer so astronomers can study it. Radio telescopes reveal information about a planet, such as its temperature and how it moves. In the search for extraterrestrials, scientists watch for specific, repeating signals. The SETI Institute and the University of California, Berkeley, built the Allen Telescope Array in 2007. The array includes 42 telescopes that work together to create a single, very powerful telescope.

Optical Telescopes

Modern **optical** telescopes allow astronomers to learn even more about what lies beyond our planet. **Laser** SETI is the latest SETI Institute optical project. The project will use special cameras placed around the world to search for flashes of light in space. Laser emissions can travel over vast distances and carry a lot of information. Ideally, the cameras will operate all the time. This way, if any signal comes in, SETI scientists will know about it.

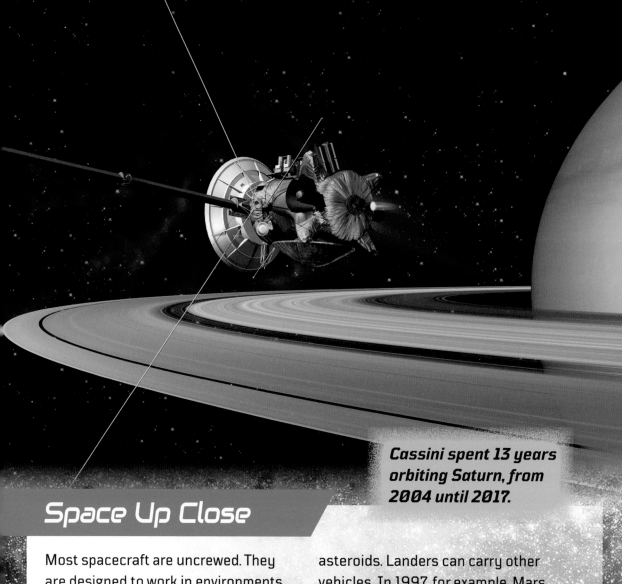

Cassini spent 13 years orbiting Saturn, from 2004 until 2017.

Space Up Close

Most spacecraft are uncrewed. They are designed to work in environments that humans would currently find difficult or even impossible to survive. Different types of **robotic** spacecraft have different uses.

Landers

Landers do just what their name suggests. They land on the surfaces of other planets, moons, comets, and asteroids. Landers can carry other vehicles. In 1997, for example, Mars Pathfinder also carried the first rover to travel across the surface of Mars. Airbags inflated before the landing to protect the lander. The Cassini **orbiter** carried the Huygens probe to Saturn and its moons. Cassini carried 12 different instruments for studying the planet and its moons. Huygens landed on the moon Titan.

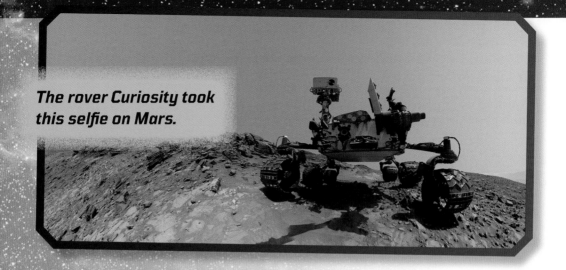

The rover Curiosity took this selfie on Mars.

Huygens is round and measures about 9 feet (2.7 m) wide. It has an outer shell that protects its instruments. The instruments include a device that can sense if a moon's surface is solid or liquid. Cassini found lakes of liquid methane and ethane on Titan. It also gathered information about Saturn's many other moons, such as Enceladus.

Rovers

Rovers travel on wheels and carry instruments for investigating. The Mars rover Sojourner was about the size of a small suitcase. The next two rovers on Mars, Spirit and Opportunity, were larger and explored different parts of the planet. Curiosity, the largest rover so far, is about the size of a car. It landed on Mars in 2012 to look for signs of life. It has 10 instruments onboard, including a computer, and 17 cameras. It is powered by batteries and **solar panels** that get energy from the Sun. It also carries **spectrometers**, which are instruments that gather information about what the rocks and air are made from.

MISSION:
Space Science

Scientists use a method called **spectroscopy** to study a planet's atmosphere. Spectroscopy splits electromagnetic radiation into wavelengths. Different wavelengths show up as different colors. Chemical elements create black gaps in the range of colors. The gaps allow scientists to figure out the chemicals in an exoplanet's atmosphere. The presence of methane or oxygen might be signs of life.

Many spacecraft do not land at all. They perform a flyby of another planet or moon. The NASA probes Voyager 1 and 2 were launched in 1977 and have been traveling in space ever since. The two spacecraft explored some of the planets in our Solar System, and Voyager 1 became the first spacecraft ever to leave our Solar System. The craft carry cameras and other instruments. The Voyager mission has given scientists a huge amount of information. Pictures of Jupiter's moon, Europa, for example, suggested that there was water under the surface.

This spacecraft image of Europa shows its cracked icy surface, which looks a bit like a cracked eggshell.

Space Telescopes

Thousands of artificial satellites are in orbit around Earth. Satellites have antennae that send and receive information, such as TV signals. They are carried into orbit by rockets. Astronomers use satellites to detect different kinds of waves from space, such as infrared light.

Telescopes carried on satellites are called space telescopes. Different space telescopes have a number of purposes and collect different kinds of information. Telescopes such as the Hubble Space Telescope (HST) are large satellites. The HST was the first large optical space telescope. It operates with large mirrors and six cameras. Its sensors can "see" visible and ultraviolet light, as well as some infrared light. It also has a **coronograph**, a device that blocks out a star's direct light so the camera can take images of nearby objects. The HST has provided information about the size and age of the universe.

dust

The HST photographed huge columns of dust where new stars are being created.

Unlike the HST, Kepler has focused on one area of space. It is much smaller than the HST and carries 42 camera sensors that can detect an exoplanet transiting, or crossing, the face of a star. Another space telescope, Spitzer, detects infrared light, or heat. It carries an infrared camera and a spectrograph. Spitzer was the first telescope to detect light from exoplanets.

Getting better images will help in the search for extraterrestrial life. The future James Webb Space Telescope (JWST) will have a mirror more than twice the size of the HST. The High Definition Space Telescope is still at the design stage. It will cost billions of dollars to build. The telescope's design includes 36 mirror segments, which will make its images sharper than any so far.

YOUR MISSION

NASA and other space agencies sometimes perform experiments in space. Can you think of any advantages that might come from being in a weightless environment? What sort of experiments would you perform there if you could? How would you go about it?

Strange Sightings

Have extraterrestrials visited Earth? Could they even be walking among us? Many people claim to have spotted extraterrestrial spacecraft in the sky. Others think there may be alien operations here on Earth.

Flying Saucers

Reports of visits by extraterrestrial beings and unidentified flying objects (UFOs) go back to ancient times. However, reported UFO sightings became common in the mid-1900s, especially in the United States.

Roswell, New Mexico, became famous as the site of an alleged UFO landing.

In 1947, Kenneth Arnold was flying his small plane near Mount Rainier, in Washington state. He claimed to see nine glowing, blue objects flying through the sky. Arnold thought the aircraft were performing some kind of military exercise. However, the U.S. military denied testing any new aircraft. That same summer, a rancher and his son found bits of tinfoil, rubber, and other materials near Roswell, New Mexico. The newspapers reported that the rancher had found the wreckage of a type of a disklike UFO called a flying saucer. Officers from the local army base became involved. The U.S. government later admitted it had been testing special balloons in the area.

Many stories of UFOs describe flying saucers. Engineers on Earth have never built such aircraft.

The balloons turned out to be part of a top-secret government operation, Project Mogul. The official government report did not come out for many years. In the meantime, Roswell became a tourist attraction. Today, people can go on tours of the crash site and visit the UFO Museum.

Around the World

After these first stories came out, many more people claimed to have seen UFOs. Some stories claimed that aliens had left their spacecraft and were living on Earth. Most of these tales came from the United States, but there were also reports from other parts of the world. In 1967, a man in Manitoba, Canada, claimed that he saw two spacecraft hovering in the sky. One landed in the woods and the other flew away. He said that the door opened and he heard sounds. Then, he claimed, the door closed and a hot vent burned his chest.

In 1989, people in Belgium reported seeing a large, triangle-shaped flying object with lights underneath. The next year, many more reports came in. This time, people claimed to see a group of these objects. Despite these many claims, science does not back them up.

In 1948, the U.S. government began to investigate reports about extraterrestrial visits. The U.S. Air Force created Project Sign. Researchers collected many reports, but one stood out. Two airline pilots reported seeing a large, fast-moving, tube-shaped object. People in the Netherlands reported seeing a similar object a few days before. The pilots drew diagrams of what they had seen. In 1949, Project Grudge took over. Its aim was to calm people's fears about extraterrestrial visits. The government reported that the sightings were likely of Soviet aircraft or natural **phenomena**, such as **meteors**, which are falling space rocks.

Keeping Track

Even so, reports of UFOs continued. In response, the U.S. Air Force began Project Blue Book. The researchers investigated UFO sightings from 1948 to 1969. During that time, there were 12,618 reported sightings. After investigation, most of these turned out to be aircraft or natural phenomena. When the government stopped the project in 1969, 701 sightings were still unexplained. In Canada, the Department of National Defense began collecting UFO reports in 1947. The National Research Council took over from 1968 to 1995. UFO monitoring still goes on around the world today.

Is it possible that some reports of UFOs are in fact sightings of top-secret high-altitude U.S. spy planes?

Most monitoring organizations are based in the United States. They include the Mutual UFO Network, which began in 1969, and the Center for UFO Studies, founded in 1973. No investigations have resulted in any proof that UFOs exist.

Area 51

The U.S. Air Force owns a large area in the desert of southern Nevada known as Area 51. Its official name is Air Force Flight Test Center. Like most military sites, it is heavily guarded. In the 1950s, the Air Force used the site to test spy planes. Because the government did not reveal the site's true purpose, some people began imagining stories. They claimed extraterrestrial spacecraft had landed or crash-landed there.

Until 2013, information about Area 51 remained classified. Even today, the military continues to use the site and some of its activities remain top secret.

Area 51 takes its name from its label on the official Air Force map of the United States.

YOUR MISSION

Imagine you were in charge of a secret program to meet aliens on Earth. In what type of location would you choose to land their spacecraft so that it would not be discovered? What questions would you ask the aliens upon meeting them?

There are many stories about aliens on Earth. Sometimes, the stories feature extraterrestrials living on Earth. Others involve people going aboard an extraterrestrial spacecraft. Most of these stories come from books, movies, and TV shows. Some of them, however, come from people who claim to have seen extraterrestrials up close.

Extraterrestrial Beings

What do aliens look like? Most people say that they have seen short, two-legged aliens with large eyes and silver, tan, or blue bodies. These aliens are known as "grays." Other people describe aliens that look like reptiles, while some say that extraterrestrials look a lot like humans. People are familiar with different ideas about extraterrestrials from movies, such as *Close Encounters of the Third Kind*, *E.T.*, or the more recent *Arrival*. Extraterrestrial characters also appear in many TV shows, including cartoons. All of these representations have an effect on people's imaginations.

One of the most common images of an alien is of a short humanoid, or human-shaped creature, with large eyes.

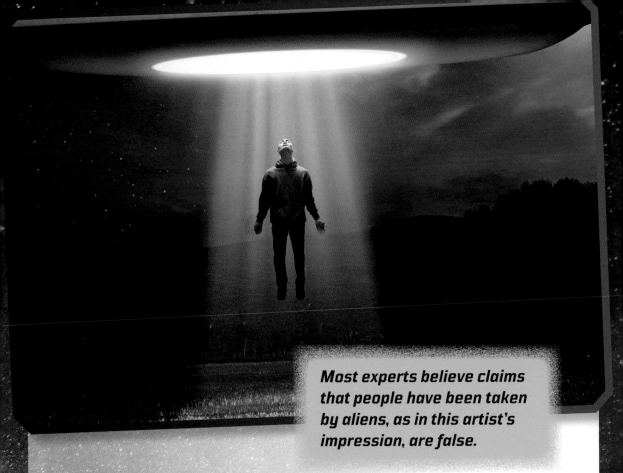

Most experts believe claims that people have been taken by aliens, as in this artist's impression, are false.

Kidnapped!

One of the most famous stories of extraterrestrials and humans comes from 1961. Americans Betty and Barney Hill described seeing a strange vehicle while driving home from vacation. They stopped their car and took a closer look. Barney said he saw alien creatures staring through the windows. The Hills got back in their car and drove off in a hurry. When they got home, they realized that there were two hours they could not remember. They were convinced that the extraterrestrials had taken them onboard their spaceship. Many other people have reported similar stories since then.

The Science

Most scientists agree that extraterrestrial sightings are false. **Psychologists** are people who study the human mind and behavior. Many psychologists believe people have dreamed or imagined meeting aliens. Books, movies, and other people's stories may have affected them.

What's Next?

The next step in finding life in space will likely be the Nexus for Exoplanet System Science (NExSS) project. The program brings together astrobiologists, astronomers, engineers, and other researchers. NExSS teams will study exoplanets to see where life could develop. NExSS will also develop new tools for the search for extraterrestrial life.

Breakthrough

In January 2016, the search for extraterrestrials got a huge boost. A new $100 million program called Breakthrough Listen began at the SETI Research Center at the University of California, Berkeley. Breakthrough Listen's main goal is the search for intelligent life. The project is using large telescopes to scan the skies.

Could the NExSS scientists one day discover a species similar to humans living on an exoplanet?

When Earth was created, conditions were very harsh—and yet life evolved there. The same might happen on other planets.

One thing the telescopes will look for are "fast radio bursts." These are high-energy flashes of light radiation from far beyond our galaxy. In tiny fractions of a second, these bursts produce as much energy as our Sun does in one day. Many likely come from natural events, such as stars colliding. However, these signals come from many light-years away. According to Breakthrough Listen, the closest fast radio burst came from 1.6 billion light-years away. SETI scientists wonder if the signals are being sent on purpose, perhaps by an extraterrestrial spacecraft. As we build larger, more sensitive radio telescopes, we may discover much more.

More Programs

Other Breakthrough programs include Breakthrough Watch and Breakthrough Starshot. The Watch program will develop technologies to help search for extraterrestrial life. Starshot is a $100 million research and engineering program. It is figuring out how a mission could reach Alpha Centauri, our nearest star, in 20 years. This is impossible now, but Starshot is trying to develop a "**nanocraft**." This small spacecraft would be powered by a laser and travel up to 100 million miles an hour (160 million kph).

Space telescopes, from the HST to TESS, are still collecting information. These missions could still reveal amazing discoveries. It is hoped that backup missions and future projects will increase our knowledge of the universe even more. Much of this exploration is aimed at searching for signs of extraterrestrial life.

Future Telescopes

Many new telescopes are being built or are planned. One of the first to be ready will be the powerful JWST. NASA, ESA, and the Canadian Space Agency (CSA) are working together on it. The telescope should launch in 2021. It is specially designed to observe infrared wavelengths and has a mirror system made up of 18 different parts. It is six times larger than the HST. The powerful JWST can observe up to 100 objects at once. The information it collects should tell scientists much about the physical and chemical nature of many exoplanets and other objects in space. The telescope will be able to follow up on information collected by TESS and other missions.

The JWST took 20 years to build. This awe-inspiring device is one of the most powerful telescopes ever built.

Other projects are being planned around the world. MeerKAT, in South Africa, is a sensitive radio telescope with 64 mirrors. It will become part of the Square Kilometer Array (SKA), based in South Africa and Australia.

Curiosity drilled this hole in a Martian rock. ExoMars will be able to drill far deeper into the surface.

Other new instruments include the PLANETS Foundation's ExoLife Finder, or ELF, a telescope that will create surface maps of exoplanets. The Foundation is also building the Polarized Light from Atmospheres of Nearby ExtraTerrestrial Systems (PLANETS) telescope. PLANETS will study the atmospheres and surfaces of exoplanets, and pick up biosignatures. The telescope will sit on a 10,000-foot (3,048-m) volcano on the island of Maui, Hawaii. The Colossus telescope, when it is built, will be even larger.

New Rover

The ExoMars mission is a new Mars rover. The rover is a joint project of ESA and Roscosmos (the Russian national space agency). Radiation would damage anything organic on the planet's surface, so ExoMars will carry a drill that can search deep underground. Curiosity has already found some microbes under the surface, but ExoMars may find even more evidence of extraterrestrial life.

Your Space Science Mission

As this book has shown you, searching for extraterrestrial life is not a simple task. There is so much for scientists to consider. They have to find planets that have the right conditions for life. They also have to be ready to find life that they may not understand. Engineers must find a way to explore planets that are many light-years away.

In this book, you have learned about some of the current exploration tools that are useful in the search for alien life. You have also read about past and future missions, on Earth and on other planets and moons. Now it's your turn to join the search! Design your own mission that might help scientists to answer one of the biggest questions of all: what might be out there?

If you could design your own spacecraft, what would it carry? Try drawing an image of how it might look.

$\alpha = 3.50113$

i

$A = bc^2$

1 2 3

Planning Your Mission

Space missions need careful planning and research. Here are some ideas and things to think about to make sure your mission will be out of this world!

1 Decide what you are looking for.
Is your mission going to look for any signs of extraterrestrial life? Or are you more of a SETI scientist who is focused on intelligent life? Knowing what you are looking for will help you design your mission.

2 Design a spacecraft.
Read about spacecraft, telescopes, and other instruments that scientists are using already. Think about ways that your design could improve on what is already being used. Could you travel farther or faster, for example?

3 Plan what needs to go onboard.
You will probably need to carry testing equipment, computers, and cameras. What kinds would be the most useful to you? Think about power and making sure your spacecraft has enough energy to get it where it needs to go.

4 Decide on a message.
If your mission is going to encounter intelligent life, you should consider sending a message. What would you include in your message and what form would it take? Read about the Golden Record sent on Voyager. That was sent a long time ago and there may be new things you want extraterrestrials to know about Earth.

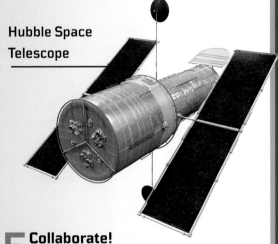

Hubble Space Telescope

5 Collaborate!
Searching for extraterrestrials is all about collaboration. Astrobiologists, astrophysicists, engineers, and others all work together. They share information and ideas. Talk to friends about your mission. See what they can add to make your mission even better.

Glossary

Please note: Some **bold-faced** words are defined where they appear in the book.

acidic Chemically harmful

amplifiers Devices that make radio signals stronger

antennae Radio aerials

atmosphere A ball of gas surrounding a planet

carbon An element that occurs in all living things

civilizations Societies with a high level of social development

colonies Communities of living things

crater A large, bowl-shaped dent in the ground

dehydrated With all moisture removed

electromagnetic Describes a magnetic field produced by an electric current

element A substance that cannot be broken down chemically

evolution The process by which things change over time

galaxy A collection of gas, dust, stars, and their solar systems

gravity A force that causes things to move toward each other

intelligent life Life forms that are able to think and communicate

laser A narrow, highly concentrated light beam

light-year The distance light travels in a year; about 5.9 trillion miles (9.5 trillion km)

microbes Tiny organisms

minerals Hard, naturally occurring substances

multicellular Many-celled

observatory A building or spacecraft for looking at space

optical Relating to light

orbiter A spacecraft that circles a planet or moon

organic Relating to living material

organisms Living things

phenomena Events that can be observed

planets Bodies in space that orbit stars

prime numbers Numbers that can only be divided by themselves and 1

radiation A type of energy

red dwarf A small, old, relatively cool star

robotic Describes a machine that performs mechanical tasks

rovers Vehicles for traveling over land

satellite A natural or artificial object that orbits a planet or star

solar panels Panels that collect sunlight to use as energy

spectrum A scale between two extremes

tubeworms Tubelike ocean creatures

Books

Aguilar, David A. *Alien Worlds: Your Guide to Extraterrestrial Life*
(National Geographic Kids). National Geographic Children's Books, 2013.

Brake, Mark. *The Alien Hunter's Handbook*. Kingfisher Children's Books, 2012.

Hawksett, David. *Extraterrestrials: Can You Find Them in the Universe?*
(Be a Space Scientist!). PowerKids Press, 2018.

Hile, Lori. *Aliens and UFOs: Myth or Reality?* (Investigating Unsolved
Mysteries). Capstone Press, 2018.

Walker, Kathryn. *Mysteries of Alien Visitors and Abductions* (Unsolved!).
Crabtree Publishing Company, 2008.

Walker, Kathryn. *Mysteries of UFOs* (Unsolved!). Crabtree Publishing
Company, 2008.

Websites

See how NASA's space missions relate to astrobiology at this site:
astrobiology.nasa.gov/missions

This "travel" site offers a virtual tour of some Earthlike exoplanets:
exoplanets.nasa.gov/alien-worlds/exoplanet-travel-bureau

Want to learn about all aspects of space exploration, including all about
exoplanets? Try this website:
spaceplace.nasa.gov/other-solar-systems/en

A page all about Mars for young readers:
mars.nasa.gov/participate/funzone

Try this NASA graphic magazine for a fun introduction to astrobiology:
www.astrobio.net/pdffiles/graphic_pdfs/Issue1_Astrobiology2.pdf

Index

About the Author

Cynthia O'Brien has written many nonfiction books for children and young readers, from science and history through to geography, space, and travel.